An Introduction to Coping with
Paranoid Thoughts

An Introduction to Coping with
Paranoid Thoughts

Katie Pownell and May Sarsam

ROBINSON

ROBINSON

First published in Great Britain in 2022 by Robinson

1 3 5 7 9 10 8 6 4 2

Copyright © Katie Pownell and May Sarsam, 2022

The moral right of the author has been asserted.

Important note
This book is not intended as a substitute for medical advice or
treatment. Any person with a condition requiring medical attention
should consult a qualified medical practitioner or suitable therapist.

A CIP catalogue record for this book
is available from the British Library.

ISBN: 978-1-47214-720-2

Typeset in Bembo by Initial Typesetting Services, Edinburgh
Printed and bound in Great Britain by Clays Ltd, Elcograf S.p.A.

Papers used by Robinson are from well-managed forests
and other responsible sources.

Robinson
An imprint of
Little, Brown Book Group
Carmelite House
50 Victoria Embankment
London EC4Y 0DZ

An Hachette UK Company
www.hachette.co.uk

www.littlebrown.co.uk

Contents

About this book

We can all feel suspicious or mistrustful at times, especially when we have gone through difficult experiences. Occasionally though, these feelings can be difficult to shake off, and can start to impact on our day-to-day lives and the lives of those around us. If this is something you can relate to, then this self-help guide could be for you.

The aim of this book is to help you to find some relief from suspicious or paranoid ideas, by offering an insight into how paranoid thoughts develop, what keeps them going, and how you can help yourself to overcome them. It uses cognitive behavioural therapy (CBT), which is a psychological treatment with a proven track record of helping people who are struggling with paranoid thinking. The approach is practical and down to earth and contains case examples that you will hopefully find useful and relevant to your own situation.

To get the most out of this book, rather than simply reading through the pages, we strongly encourage you to take part in the exercises, and to use these opportunities to pause, take a step back and reflect. This can be challenging and may be different to how you have managed up until now; however the very fact that you have picked this book up shows that you might be ready to make some changes – that is a great first step!

The idea of being open to looking at your situation differently can be daunting, and trying out new things may feel strange at first. However, developing and adopting new strategies is important in moving forward and finding some relief, and putting new learning into practice is key. It's OK if you find yourself slipping back into old habits alongside the new ones that this book introduces you to: it's all part of learning. Try to remain open to these new experiences and see what happens – you won't regret it!

This book is designed for you to use as a form of self-help. However, if you find that you are not making as much progress as you would like or if you require additional support, please take a look at the Useful Resources section at the end of this book. There you will find books that give a little more detail on the topics discussed. If at any time you feel worse, or are struggling, remember there is help available for you. This may include visiting your GP or speaking to another healthcare worker about how you are feeling. You are not alone, and you can do this!

Good luck!

May Sarsam and Katie Pownell

Part 1: UNDERSTANDING PARANOID THOUGHTS

1

What is Paranoia?

We have probably all come across the term 'paranoia'. It is a commonly used word because paranoid thoughts are quite common. Paranoia is the experience of feeling strongly suspicious or mistrustful about people, things or the world, when most other people around us do not feel there is a good enough reason to feel that way. It can involve us holding beliefs that others are trying to harm us in some way, or are talking about us, laughing at us, know things about us, or are planning something against us. The beliefs can be very strong, and people who are experiencing paranoia can feel that they are absolutely true, beyond a shadow of a doubt. Even if we have an awareness that our paranoia might not be entirely based in reality, the thoughts can be incredibly distressing, and can have a major impact on our quality of life.

Common examples of paranoid thoughts are:

- people are talking or laughing about you behind your back

- others are trying to harm you in some way

- you are at risk of being harmed, or your life is in danger

- people are deliberately trying to trick, upset or annoy you

- you are being watched or targeted by other people or agencies

- people are trying to steal from you in some way

- others are using double meanings to threaten you

Research has shown that paranoid thinking happens across a range or 'continuum', with very common experiences at one end, like suspiciousness when something unusual happens, to very strongly held, specific beliefs at the other, less common end, for example thinking that someone intends to do you serious harm.

The intensity of the paranoid thoughts can also range from mild to severe. For most people, the thoughts might come and go quickly; we can dismiss them without too much effort, and they cause little distress or impact on our lives. For some people however, the thoughts really bother us; they stick around, we tend to spend a long time paying attention to them and they can start to have a big impact on our day-to-day functioning.

It is important to consider whether our thoughts might be accurate, and based on real concerns, evidence or threats. How can we tell? Beliefs are described as 'paranoid' when they don't seem to fit in with what other people around us think is a reasonable concern, even when those other people have access to the same information or evidence that we do. Paranoia becomes a problem when those thoughts, concerns and beliefs start to get in the way of us living a normal life.

Paranoid thoughts tend to involve four elements:

- something harmful could happen to us or those we care about

- someone or something is deliberately intending to cause that harm

- the idea is difficult to dismiss and keeps coming up

- other people around us don't agree with our assessment of what is happening

Intensity: how much does the belief impact on your mood or day-to-day life?

Severe impact

Moderate impact

Little or no impact

3

2

1

4

Extremely common
E.g. superstitions held by many of the general public, or being more watchful after hearing about local crime

Less common
E.g. conspiracy theories – held by a minority of people

Even less common
E.g. beliefs about being at imminent risk of harm – held by a few

Commonality: how common is it for people to have thoughts or beliefs like this?

Cross 1: Frank believes black cats are unlucky. He feels so worried about this that if he sees one, he experiences anxiety and sleepless nights, worrying about what might happen. The idea that black cats might be unlucky is very common to lots of people, but Frank's belief is strong enough to cause a moderate impact on his mood and life (anxiety and sleeplessness) so his cross is towards the left-hand side and halfway up the graph.

Cross 2: Andy believes the Moon landing was faked. He has watched a number of documentaries on it and is convinced that this is the case, making him suspicious of governments generally. Andy's belief does not get in the way of his job or his relationships. It doesn't bother him from day to day, although he does spend a lot of time researching and sharing his ideas on internet groups. His belief is less common but does not impact his life or mood very much, so his cross is in the centre-bottom of the graph.

Cross 3: For the last three months, Gisele has believed that she is in danger of being hurt by a man who shouted at her in the pub she used to work at. Following this incident, Gisele became very upset and frightened. She quit her job for fear that he might look for her there and has begun to worry that he has found out where she lives. Her colleagues, friends, family and the police don't believe there is any reason for Gisele to worry about her safety, but Gisele is unconvinced. She is frequently tearful, has panic attacks most days and will not leave the house. Gisele's belief is not a common one to have, and it has understandably had a major impact on her mood and day-to-day life. Her cross is therefore in the top right section of the graph.

Cross 4: Chris hears that cars in the local area have been broken into and worries that his car might be at risk. For the next few weeks, Chris parks his car in view of his bedroom window, makes sure to remove all visible items at the end of every day, and checks the car from his window a couple of times every evening. His concern is very common and understandable, and is not impacting negatively on his life, so his cross is in the lower left-hand corner.

Andy's beliefs about the Moon landing don't impact his life, or the lives of those around him, so there is really no need for him to change anything about it if that's what he chooses to believe. Similarly, Chris's suspicious belief that car theft would not be considered problematic. For Frank and Gisele, however, their beliefs are upsetting for them and are routinely affecting their lives from day to day, so it may be useful for them if those beliefs could change so that they impact their lives a little less.

2

Who Experiences Paranoia?

We can all be mistrustful at times, particularly if life hasn't treated us well. Anyone who has been burgled will be familiar with the lingering worries we might have about noises in the house that can happen for some time afterwards. Or that thought when you have got a puncture for the third time in a month that maybe someone is leaving nails near your car. This is part of our brain's threat monitoring system and is completely normal. If we have been through something unpleasant or difficult, our brains will be working extra hard to look out for danger next time. Without even noticing, we may end up thinking that it is better to 'err on the side of caution' and assume something is dangerous rather than not, if that means that we avoid any potential harm. This completely normal brain process is what's behind that experience of worrying a great deal about something for a few days or weeks, but eventually realising we had got the wrong end of the stick. For example, the noises we have been hearing at night turn out to be pigeons in the loft, or we find out that the nails in the road were dropped by our neighbour's builders.

Around 10–15 per cent of us experience paranoid thoughts on a regular basis. As explained earlier, these thoughts only become problematic when they are not easy to dismiss and start to have a significant impact on our lives. There are certain conditions that make this more likely to happen for us, and paranoia is more commonly described by people who have had or are currently experiencing:

- poor sleep

- trauma or difficult life experiences

- victimisation or bullying

- social isolation

- anxiety or worry

- stress

- a natural tendency to make decisions quickly

Paranoia can be a sign of stress, or a symptom of a mental health issue such as depression, anxiety or psychosis, but it is not a mental health diagnosis itself, and it involves complex thinking processes. Let's look at some of the ways in which paranoia can become a problem for us.

Poor sleep

Having a couple of nights of poor sleep will not usually have much of an impact on most of us, however if we miss out on sleep more regularly, it can take its toll on our emotional wellbeing. Those of us who have experienced periods of poor sleep might already be familiar with how it can have an impact on our mood. We can become more irritable, anxious, stressed or impatient than usual. Regular lack of sleep can start to put us in a more negative frame of mind. We might also notice that when we are tired it is harder to think clearly and make sense of things around us as easily, and this can leave us feeling unsettled or unsure of things. The world can seem different when we are sleep-deprived, and often in a negative way. It is not uncommon for people to notice unusual thoughts, and for some people, this can be when they first start to notice suspicious or paranoid ideas. Research studies have shown that extreme sleep deprivation can even lead people to experience hallucinations.

Trauma, difficult life experiences, victimisation and bullying

Paranoia is more common in people who have faced adversity, abuse or trauma in their lives. Being exposed to such difficult experiences can sometimes leave us struggling with our self-esteem, and this might make us feel vulnerable. We may also have learned that the world can be a dangerous or unfair place, and because we have had direct experience of people causing us harm or letting us down, we may well find it difficult to trust others. If we are this way inclined, it is understandable that we might be more likely to adopt a more cautious approach when faced with an uncertain or ambiguous situation, being more inclined to jump to the worst-case scenario in order to try and keep ourselves safe. This is also seen in people who have been bullied, victimised or treated differently to those around them. Again, very understandably, such experiences can result in a tendency to look out for danger in social situations. In turn, this could lead us to overestimate threat in social situations and interactions with others, whether there may be actual danger or not.

If we have had difficult experiences during our childhood, this effect can be even more pronounced. This is because adversity early in life can, over time, lead to differences in how the nervous system develops. The nervous system is responsible for managing how we respond to threat, and if we have experienced lots of threat or danger early in life, we can become stuck in a 'threat alertness' state, meaning that we are on guard, or feel we might be in danger much of the time. Because our threat systems are overactive, we are more likely to notice, and be sensitive to, a perceived threat, and to have a big emotional response to it – even if the actual chance of danger is very small. This can be understandably exhausting.

Social isolation

Social isolation and loneliness have been linked to paranoia. Some reasons suggested by research are that people who are socially isolated may view themselves, others and their environment in a more negative light than those with a strong social network, and may also feel a sense of powerlessness, and disconnection from their community. Without the 'social safety' we feel from having people around us who we know and trust, we may be more likely to have a global view of the world as unsafe or threatening, which can lead some people towards experiencing paranoid thoughts.

Anxiety and worry

If we are experiencing anxiety and worry, our brains are focused on coping with some kind of threat or danger. This could be the threat of not having enough money to pay our bills, or of failing our exams, or of becoming ill. When we spend a long time focused on threat, our brains can become accustomed to thinking that way. This makes it more likely that we will predict or expect danger, whether there is a real danger or not. Furthermore, people who have lived with anxiety for a long time can develop a belief that spending time worrying is important and useful in order to predict and avoid danger. The problem with this is that worrying can lead to us coming up with all sorts of plausible, but also implausible, ideas. Anxiety and worry can therefore sometimes contribute to the development of paranoid ideas.

Stress

Stress plays a big role in the development and maintenance of all mental health difficulties, and its importance in the development of paranoia is no different. When psychologists talk about stress, they are not only thinking of work-related pressure or arguments at home, but also lots of other things we might not consider, like bereavements, caring responsibilities, the environmental stress of living somewhere very noisy or chaotic, as well as the stress of experiencing boredom, loneliness or depression, among other things. Even things that most of us might consider positive, like weddings or Christmas, can be stressful whether we notice it or not. Human beings are generally good at coping with stress, but we all have a certain amount we can cope with before we begin to feel overwhelmed. We can think of this 'stress quota' as a bucket. If the bucket starts to get too full, this shows itself in our mental wellbeing. We may begin to feel anxious, snappy, low in mood, panicky, struggle to sleep well, or notice unusual thoughts, including paranoid thoughts. These experiences themselves are stressful, putting more stress straight back in the bucket. To try and manage all this, we may start to use strategies like drinking more alcohol, using substances, or distracting ourselves with other unhelpful habits. These also tend to add to the stress bucket rather than drain it.

The final difficulty with stress is that when we have too much of it we tend not to look after ourselves as well. We may do fewer of the things we enjoy or find relaxing, we may pay less attention to our physical wellbeing and self-care, and we may withdraw from other people, making ourselves more isolated. As we have seen above, all of these factors can impact on our likelihood of experiencing paranoia, which we know is very stressful, and so the cycle continues.

What stresses are going into the bucket?

Arguments with family

Noisy neighbours

Financial problems

Looking after kids

Background stress

Bucket overflowing
Begin to notice anxiety, low mood or panic

Stressful

Unhelpful coping
E.g. drinking too much, skipping sleep

Healthy coping
E.g. eating properly, gentle activity that helps you relax, connecting with others, creative outlets

CASE EXAMPLE: Liam

Liam is a 29-year-old man who lives alone in a block of flats. There is lots of antisocial behaviour where he lives, and his neighbour plays loud music through the night at weekends.

Liam describes his childhood as 'OK'. He gets along well with his mum, as well as his two older sisters, but he often argues with his younger brother, and so tends not to visit his family often. Liam's dad passed away when he was very young and he only has a few memories of him.

Liam has experienced low mood since his early teens, when he was bullied at school. He recalls always feeling as though he was 'different' from his peers and felt lonely growing up.

When Liam left school, he started going to the pub and drinking alcohol, and also started to experiment with recreational drugs in order to fit in with his peers. However, he now recognises that his substance use has become more of a habit.

Liam has found casual bar work in the evenings, and although this provides him with an income, he continues to struggle for money. He is finding that he is using more cocaine to get him through his shifts as sometimes he doesn't get home until 4am. He is getting behind on his rent and owes his drug dealer money, which he is struggling to pay back. He is worried about how he will repay the debt, and what might happen if he can't . . . He is very anxious and feels trapped in this situation.

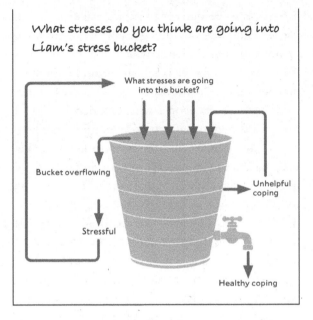

What stresses do you think are going into Liam's stress bucket?

What stresses are going into the bucket?

Bucket overflowing

Unhelpful coping

Stressful

Healthy coping

A natural tendency to make decisions quickly

Research has shown that some individuals who go on to develop problematic paranoid thoughts have more of a tendency to 'jump to conclusions', in that they tend to make decisions or judgements based on less information than those who do not experience so many paranoid thoughts. If we have this natural tendency, it means that we are more likely to form and hold a belief based on less evidence than most others might need to form or hold the same belief.

We may also be quicker to notice evidence which we feel supports our thoughts, while discounting or not noticing evidence which does not support them. This is another completely normal thinking process, called 'confirmation bias', which tends to be stronger in people who experience a lot of paranoid thoughts. Like many of our thinking processes, its evolutionary purpose is to keep us safe. Imagine our ancient ancestors believing that 'there might be a tiger hiding in that grass'. The ones who had a quick look around, saw the grass moving but decided it was probably just the wind, might not have lived to have many children! By contrast, the ones who looked at the moving grass and decided it probably *was* a tiger and avoided going in there, would have been less likely to get eaten, whether there actually was a tiger hiding in the grass or not.

If we hold a belief that is about keeping us safe, our brains will automatically look for evidence to back up that belief and automatically dismiss evidence that might mean we are actually safe. This helps us to understand how paranoid thoughts can end up getting stronger and stronger. Confirmation bias can also lead people to accept distorted or false memories (which might have occurred due to stress or an altered mental state, for example through lack of sleep), as evidence to confirm paranoid beliefs. Being aware of this is important as it can help us to begin to examine our thinking patterns more closely.

Paranoia can also be an added feature of:

- psychosis

- drug or alcohol use

- dementia

- epilepsy

- brain injury

Paranoid thoughts can be a feature of psychosis, which is when a person may lose some contact with reality. A person with psychosis may also be seeing or hearing things that others cannot, which can be very distressing indeed. It is important to seek help from a medical or mental health professional if you think you may be experiencing psychosis, as there are various treatments that can help.

There is some debate over how drugs and alcohol might lead to us experiencing paranoid thoughts; however, certain drugs, such as cocaine, cannabis, amphetamines and alcohol are known to trigger paranoid thinking in some people. Abstaining from alcohol and drug use may therefore be helpful if you are experiencing paranoid beliefs.

Some illnesses can lead to people experiencing paranoia too. These may include epilepsy, Parkinson's disease, Huntington's disease, strokes, brain injuries, and some forms of dementia including Alzheimer's disease. Healthcare professionals can support those presenting with these difficulties if they begin to struggle with paranoid thoughts.

3

The Impact of Paranoia

The impact of paranoia varies from person to person. Some may be able to continue as usual with their lives and find that they are only affected at certain times or in certain situations. However, for others, the paranoia becomes quite influential in their lives and limits them in a number of ways. For example, we may begin to avoid certain places or people, or may change some of our usual activities or behaviours. This can make relationships with others harder to keep going, which can leave us feeling isolated, or even result in more anxiety or worry about what others around us might be thinking.

Struggling with paranoia might also result in us feeling cut off, lonely and alone with our experiences, which can be upsetting. As well as this, having a belief that we are in danger prevents us from living our lives in the way that we would like to, which might result in us feeling sad or hopeless about the future.

Frustratingly, all these impacts can increase our stress levels considerably, which in turn can increase the frequency of our paranoid thoughts, and so again the cycle continues.

Witnessing a friend or loved one who is experiencing paranoia can take its toll. Carers might feel stuck, frustrated, worried and confused, mirroring how the person themselves is sometimes feeling. If we know someone who is experiencing a lot of paranoid thoughts, we might also be unsure about how to respond to them, especially if we do not agree with or share the beliefs the person is having. We might feel a pressure to go along with the person's ideas in order to help reassure them that they are not 'crazy'. We might feel the need to challenge them, which could lead to conflict or risk losing their trust. Or we might feel it is better to avoid them altogether in order not to make things worse. It can be a confusing choice. If we are living with someone who is experiencing a lot of paranoid ideas, we may also find our own lives becoming more and more limited by their attempts to stay safe, we might find ourselves becoming more isolated as a result, and it might be difficult to see a way forward.

CASE EXAMPLE: Natalie and Pete

Natalie is aged 17 and has been attending college for the last year. She went to a different college to most of her school friends and has always felt shy when it comes to meeting new people. As a result, she struggled to make new friends in college and felt quite left out. One day in class about six months ago, Natalie heard the girls behind her whispering and giggling, but couldn't quite hear what they were saying; she tried to ignore it but felt that they must have been laughing at her. Later that week, Natalie went to the canteen for lunch and noticed the same girls look up at her when she entered the room and then they laughed as she walked past them. Natalie felt on edge, and instead of getting her lunch, she went home from college saying that she felt unwell.

Since that time, Natalie's attendance at college has been poor. When she does attend, Natalie often thinks that other students are talking about her or laughing at her, and she struggles to concentrate in her lessons. She does not talk to anyone unless she must, and eats lunch on her own in a quiet corner of the library. One of Natalie's tutors was concerned because Natalie's grades were suffering and asked her what was wrong. Natalie told him about the other students talking about her and laughing at her, and he tried to reassure her that there was nothing to worry about; however, this did not help and led to Natalie feeling even more embarrassed. As a result, Natalie has now not been to college for three weeks and is at risk of being excluded.

Natalie lives with her dad, Pete, who is very worried about his daughter, having noticed a big change in her over the last five or six months. Natalie used to have a group of friends from school who she would see in the evenings and at weekends, and she was always a very good student. When Natalie first started to miss college, Pete tried to support her to attend and was late for work himself on a few occasions, after spending extra time reassuring and encouraging Natalie. This led to Pete receiving a written warning from his boss. When Pete tried to reassure Natalie that the other students are not talking about her, this caused them to argue and, on one occasion, Natalie accused Pete of being on the 'side' of the other students. They both got upset and ended up shouting at each other.

Over time, Pete has begun to feel exhausted and at a loss about how to help Natalie. Now he leaves Natalie to her own devices and only knocks on her bedroom door to offer her meals. Pete feels like he is a failure as a father and is struggling with low mood himself. He goes to work each day but cannot concentrate and has stopped seeing his own friends because he does not like to leave Natalie at home alone any more than he has to.

When Natalie leaves the house now, she always wears a cap pulled low over her eyes, and a hoodie with the hood pulled up. She does this so that other people don't recognise her, and will go out like this even on a hot day. She is very watchful and makes a mental note of everyone she sees when she is out. The kids in her neighbourhood have started calling her 'a freak' for wearing a hoodie in the summer. Hearing these nasty things has left Natalie feeling even more targeted and self-conscious.

Natalie would like to get a job but does not feel confident enough to look for work. Pete wishes his daughter could find a way through this so they can go out for lunch together like they used to.

4

Understanding Threat Beliefs

Research suggests that paranoia tends to happen more when we are already worried about some kind of threat. This could be a physical threat of harm, a fear of what other people think of us or of what intentions other people have towards us. People who don't have a particular worry or fear, called a 'threat belief', tend not to notice paranoid thoughts very often, or if they do they are easy to dismiss.

Threat beliefs may develop from our earlier experiences. If we have been threatened, hurt or abused by other people, we are more likely to develop negative beliefs about ourselves, others or the world around us. We are not always aware of the beliefs we hold, and they are not necessarily true; however, they *feel* very true to us as they are based on previous experience. They can drive our thoughts, feelings and behaviour too; for example, if someone has the belief that 'the world is a dangerous place' they may *think* that other people are out to hurt them, making them *feel* frightened, and they may therefore be more watchful for any signs that others are intending them harm. Ultimately, these beliefs are there to protect us from harm – emotional and physical. However, if left unchecked, it is easy to see how they might begin to get in the way of us living the life we want to live.

When a 'threat belief' is present, the natural thing for a person to do is to try to keep themselves safe. Let's return to the 'tiger in the grass' example from earlier in the book. The way we try to keep ourselves safe from a potential tiger is to look around carefully for any sign of tigers. This is the same for any threat belief – we all tend to look around carefully for signs of the thing we are worried about.

Do you ever find yourself watching things around you and checking for something?

....

....

....

Remember, to help make sure we spot any signs of danger or threat, our brains will tend to ignore any information that isn't threatening and concentrate very hard on the information that *might* be threatening (confirmation bias).

The problem with this is that we *don't notice the signs that we might be safe*. And the problem with concentrating on being watchful is that if we look hard enough, we can find evidence for anything! Because of this, if we are experiencing a lot of paranoid thoughts, we can feel strongly that something that most other people would think of as completely innocent is evidence that our threat belief is true.

For example, let's think about the example of Natalie from the previous chapter. Natalie is walking down a quiet street and sees three young people walking along, chatting to themselves, joking and laughing.

If Natalie has a threat belief that everybody talks about her when she is out, how watchful would she be of the people walking towards her? What might she notice? How might she feel?

....

....

....

If Natalie is busy listening to her music and thinking about what she is going to cook for dinner tonight, how watchful would she be of the people walking towards her then? Would she notice as much about them? Would she feel as threatened, frightened or worried?

....

....

....

The vicious cycle of paranoia

When we are in 'threat mode' and trying to keep ourselves safe, the following four things happen to our **thinking:**

- our **threat belief** becomes **active**

- we become very **watchful** for any danger signs (which means we are very likely to find some) and **pay more attention** to these when we find them

- we tend to **ignore** anything that might mean we are not in danger

- we tend to **interpret** innocent things as threatening

This has an effect on **how we feel:**

- anxious

- frightened

- paranoid

- angry

- stressed

- mistrustful

- suspicious

And on **what we do:**

- keep checking for danger

- start to avoid people or places

All this can make the threat belief stronger and stronger, which makes us feel even more paranoid. Avoidance plays a key part in this, as the more the cycle goes on, the more we tend to avoid the things we think are threatening. This might start with not seeing certain people or not going to certain places, but over time it may be that we start to avoid more people, or more places, and eventually struggle to do very much of what we would usually do. This avoidance means that we have even less chance of noticing any evidence that we might be safe, which helps the paranoid ideas to get a stronger hold.

In the chart overleaf we can see how the arrows lead from one part of the cycle to all the others.

Look back to Natalie's case example (see page 23). Below is the vicious cycle of paranoia based on Natalie's case:

Here we can see that Natalie's **threat belief** is: 'Everyone is talking about me and laughing at me.' So, when she is in college, her **attention** is focused on watching for signs that other students are talking about her or laughing at her. She tries to overhear their conversations, is vigilant of students in her vicinity laughing or giggling, and when she goes into a classroom or the canteen, Natalie looks for people's reactions to try and work out whether they are talking about her. This is understandably very stressful, and leads to Natalie **feeling** anxious, self-conscious and isolated. In order to manage all this, Natalie modifies her **behaviour**: she avoids going to college, feeling safer at home; if she does go to college, she avoids other students in social situations, for example by eating her lunch alone in the library. This means that Natalie has very few recent examples of any positive, pleasant social interactions at college. The function of Natalie's behaviour is to try and keep herself safe; however, can you see how it may actually serve to keep the problems going?

In the next section, we will look at whether you might like to examine your own threat beliefs in a bit more detail, and there will be the option to complete your own vicious cycle like the one above.

Part 2: COPING WITH PARANOIA

5

Potential Benefits of Managing Threat Beliefs

It may feel daunting to think of questioning the way we have been looking at things for a while, particularly if we feel that viewing things in this way has kept us safe from harm. It is certainly important to keep ourselves safe, but it is equally important to check we are not limiting ourselves too much – 'just in case'.

As we have seen in previous sections, when we have very active threat beliefs it can start to impact on our attention, our feelings and our behaviour and can lead to a vicious cycle. Have a think about your own experiences since you started to be very worried about something. Look at the list of problems below and consider whether they apply to you.

Problem	Yes/No
We can end up spending a lot of time and effort trying to avoid a potential threat, even before we have checked to see if our fears are justified.	
Our emotional state can become quite negative – we spend a lot of time feeling irritable, worried, panicky or anxious. This leaves less time to feel okay, happy or content.	
We might not be sleeping very well, leaving us feeling unrefreshed and exhausted all the time.	
Our energy levels get low due to spending so much mental effort on trying to avoid the threat. We don't have much energy left for things that are productive or fun.	
Our relationships are impacted as other people find it difficult to live with our worry or behaviour, or because we don't feel safe enough to keep in contact. This can leave us feeling lonely or isolated.	

Because we are doing less and avoiding people, we have less opportunity to notice any evidence that might challenge our threat beliefs.	
We might use alcohol, substances or other unhealthy distractions to cope with the stress of the situation, which can cause their own problems in our lives.	

All of the above experiences are stressful, and what we know about threat beliefs is that they become stronger and more frequent when we are under stress. So, if we are noticing some of the signs above, we need to remember that this in itself can help strengthen those threat beliefs even more.

Even when we recognise a lot of these negative effects, it can still feel like a big step to consider doing anything about it. Weighing up the pros and cons can be helpful here: look at the tables below and put a tick next to the statements you agree with.

KEEPING THINGS AS THEY ARE

Pros	Agree	Cons	Agree
It might be easier than changing things		My life is limited by my worries	
I know what to expect		It is lonely	
My quality of life is fine		It is boring	
I feel safer this way		I am always anxious	
		My quality of life is not good	
		I feel low	
		The way things are puts me under a lot of stress	
		The way things are puts other people I care about under a lot of stress	

SAFELY CHECKING OUT MY THREAT BELIEFS

Pros	Agree	Cons	Agree
I could find out that things aren't as bad as I thought		I would be stepping out of my comfort zone	
I might be able to do more of the things I'd like to do		I might feel more anxious while I am checking things out	
Life might be less stressful		It might be upsetting to learn that I have been overcautious	
I might be able to have closer relationships		I might not succeed, which would feel like a disappointment	
The people important to me could have a better quality of life			
I could have a better quality of life			

Although it may be anxiety-provoking, the potential gains of safely checking out our threat beliefs could be worth it. **The exercises in this book will not do anything to put you at risk.** Their aim is to help you safely and securely examine your own situation, so you can decide for yourself whether your current worries are taking up too much room in your life.

Making sense of my experiences

A great first step is to write down the worries or beliefs that are getting in the way of your life at the moment.

Are there any beliefs you hold that are getting in the way of your everyday life? Write them down here.

....

....

....

Are those beliefs shared by other people around you? Family? Friends? Health workers?

....

....

....

What would it be like for you if those beliefs were not as strong as they are right now?

....

....

....

Let's take a closer look at how these beliefs might be impacting on you right now. Look back at the example on page 32. Can you fill in your own experiences here? Get someone you trust to help you with this if you are not sure.

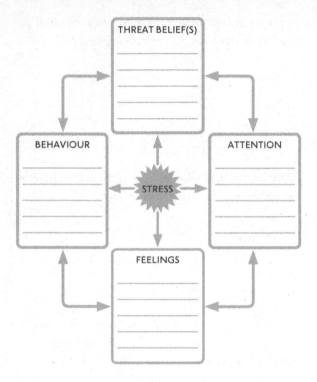

By filling in the diagram above we might have noticed the following:

- Our beliefs, attention, feelings and behaviour all influence each other.

- If we are feeling worried, unsafe or concerned, it makes us pay closer attention to the possible threat. This means we are more likely to find something to worry about.

- The four factors (see page 30) can work together to help strengthen the cycle.

- A normal response for anyone experiencing a cycle like this would be to feel stressed.

- Remember, when we are stressed, it is normal for negative thoughts to 'pop' into our heads – it is our brain's way of trying to help keep us safe, left over from the days of watching for tigers in the grass.

- This constant supply of negative thoughts helps keep the threat belief at the top of our 'worry list', using up more and more of our mental energy.

6

Checking Our Stress Levels

The first strategy for managing our threat beliefs is to check our stress levels. This is a win–win. As mentioned earlier, too much stress can stop us from thinking clearly, leading to poorer problem solving and other undesirable effects. So, if nothing else, getting a better handle on our stress levels can help us to feel better, day to day.

Research on stress has shown that there are a number of life events that are very likely to cause stress for most people – some of them might surprise us. In the following table, a 'life change unit' is a unit of measurement from 1–100 assigned to potential events in an individual's life, based on surveys carried out on the general population.

Life event	Life change units	I have experienced this
Death of a spouse / sibling / parent during our childhood	100	
Unplanned pregnancy	100	
Divorce / separation	73	
Being imprisoned	63	
Death of a close family member / friend	63	
Serious injury or illness in self / immediate family / being a victim of a crime	53	
Getting married	50	
Losing job / retirement	47	
Gaining a new family member (e.g. a new baby) / someone new moving into the home	40	
Changes at work (a promotion or any change of role)	39	

Changes in financial status (having a lot less money or a lot more)	39	
Child leaving home	29	
Family conflict	29	
Outstanding personal achievement	28	
Recently moving house/school	20	
Change in social activities	19	
Going on holiday	12	

Even if we have experienced some of these events, it does not necessarily mean we have been deeply affected by them. But it is worth checking . . . Some people find it easy to notice if they are under stress, while for others it can be less noticeable. Here are some commons signs of stress or anxiety. Tick the ones you or those close to you have noticed.

	I have noticed this sign of stress	Those close to me have noticed this in me
Poor sleep		
Headaches		
Stomach problems / pain / feeling sick		
Feeling shaky		
Feeling dizzy		
Racing thoughts / can't switch off		
Ruminating or worrying about something in particular		
Appetite changes		
Irritable / snappy		
Low motivation / can't get started		
Tired all the time		

Jumpy / easy to startle		
Heart pounding		
Unable to relax		
Feeling on edge		
Avoiding people		
Drinking more alcohol / using more substances		
Changes to sex drive		
Hard to think clearly		
On guard or watchful		
Difficulty concentrating		

A sudden increase in stress can be very significant. For example, being mugged, losing a job or breaking up with a partner can make someone feel very stressed. We may start to turn inwards and isolate ourselves more, or we may start to feel more insecure and under threat. Think about whether you were very stressed in the lead-up to first noticing your 'threat belief'. This can be an important sign.

Which stresses did you notice just before or about the same time as you started to feel worried about your 'threat belief'?

....

....

....

Think back to the stress bucket on page 15. How full do you think your stress bucket might have been at the time when you first noticed your threat beliefs?

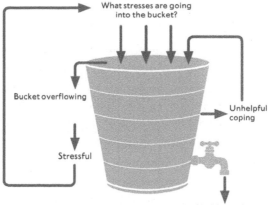

7

Managing Our Stress Levels

Once we have identified that stress might be play-ing a role, the next step is to start looking after ourselves a little better, to help drain the bucket. Here are some easy stress-management techniques you can practise using.

Mindfulness

Mindfulness is about gently but purposefully bring-ing your attention to the present moment, instead of worrying about the past or the future. It is not always useful for everyone but can sometimes be very helpful for people who struggle with racing thoughts or negative thoughts through the day. You can do mindfulness anywhere, anytime, and evidence shows that even a two-minute mindfulness exercise can make a big difference to your mood. While practising mindfulness it is perfectly normal for other thoughts or feelings to pop into our heads. When this happens, just notice them and say, 'Oh, it's a thought' or 'Oh, it's a feeling' but don't focus on them. Instead, bring yourself back to the task. Try this exercise:

- Sit comfortably in a chair with your legs and arms uncrossed, your feet resting on the ground, and your back supported.

- Bring your attention to your breath. Breathe slowly, deeply and evenly, in through your nose and out through your mouth.

- Place your hand on your tummy so you can feel it rise and fall as you breathe in and out.

- Finding your own rhythm and pace, make your out-breath last a little longer than your in-breath: breathe in for 1–2–3–4 and out for 1–2–3–4–5–6, with a little pause at the end.

- Take several breaths like this, counting to 4 on the in-breath and 6 on the out-breath as you go.

- Continue to breathe slowly, deeply and evenly, and become aware of your feet touching the floor. Notice how they feel, their temperature, the ground beneath them.

- Become aware of your hands – the one on your tummy and the other one. Notice whether they are tense or relaxed, and the sensations your fingertips are feeling.

- Become aware of your neck and shoulders. Is there tension there? As you breathe out, try to drop your shoulders a little bit and notice how that feels.

- Become aware of your face and jaw. Is there tension there? As you breathe out, try to relax your face a little bit and notice how that feels.

- Become aware of your legs and feet. Is there tension there? As you breathe out, try to relax your leg muscles a little bit and notice how that feels.

- Now notice the sound of your own breathing.

- Now notice the temperature around you.

- Now notice any smells.

- Now notice how bright or dark it is and spend a minute looking around.

You have now completed at least two minutes of mindfulness. Maybe the experience of focusing on the present for a little while has had a small positive impact on your mood. Keep practising as often as you like. Mindfulness gets easier and more effective with practice.

Distraction

Distraction is about purposefully interrupting an unhelpful or stressful train of thought by doing something else that takes up your attention. What works as a distraction is quite individual to you, but the activity you choose should be immersive enough that it is difficult to fit in 'thinking' on top of it. Here are some examples:

- Counting all the blue / red / silver objects you can see in the room around you.

- Watch videos on a subject completely new to you.

- Clear out a cupboard, a drawer or your kitchen.

- Do puzzles like sudoku, crosswords, word-searches.

- Play a demanding video game.

- Watch your favourite sport.

- Fix something in the house or garden that needs fixing.

- Write a story or a poem just for fun.

Grounding

Grounding is about using an object or smell to help interrupt persistent or distressing thoughts and feelings. Sometimes focusing on something sensory can give our brains the break they need and instantly lift our mood. Grounding objects can be anything that has a texture, weight or feel that is pleasing to you and small enough to fit into your pocket. Grounding smells should be strong, punchy and pleasant. If there is a scent you find pleasant and calming, it is very difficult to feel worse after smelling it! Breathe deeply and notice the tension reduce.

Examples of grounding objects

A smooth pebble, an interesting shell, a piece of furry or velvet fabric, a small fidget toy.

Examples of grounding smells

Lavender, rosemary, citrus fruits, essential oil, sandalwood, strawberry, mint, perfume, your favourite soap, shower gel or washing powder.

Self-soothing

Self-soothing is helpful for toning down our feelings of threat. It is about actively doing something that we find calming or relaxing. Usually this includes slow activities but it can also be things that are more high-intensity, if that is what you find relaxing.

Examples of self-soothing

Taking a long shower, reading a familiar book that you have enjoyed before, watching your favourite movie or TV show, treating yourself to your favourite food, going for a run or doing exercise you enjoy, going for a walk in nature, stroking a pet, listening to music that you find relaxing and pleasant.

Sleep and rest

The importance of sleep and rest in managing our stress levels cannot be underestimated, yet sleep is often one of the first things that suffers when we are stressed. Some sleep hygiene principles can help, and getting regular rest and sleep will definitely improve your stress levels. Have a look at the following sleep hygiene strategies.

- Avoid caffeine after 5pm.

- Switch screens off an hour before you want to go to sleep.

- Have a relaxing shower or bath.

- Do a quiet, repetitive activity like drawing or reading.

- Drink something warm and milky – this helps to release sleep hormones.

- Avoid alcohol as this tends to interrupt healthy sleep leaving you feeling unrefreshed in the morning.

- Only go to bed when you feel tired enough to sleep.

- If you are lying awake for a long time, get up and do a quiet activity (without screens) for twenty minutes before taking yourself back to bed.

If you have tried the above strategies consistently for a couple of weeks and haven't noticed an improvement, speak to your GP about a short-term supply of sleeping tablets if you are still having trouble, to help you get back into a healthy bedtime routine.

8

Examining Our Threat Beliefs
(Do Things Add Up?)

When we believe something very strongly, we tend not to question it. Instead, our brains will try to make sense of the evidence in front of us in a way that supports our beliefs. This is that survival tactic from prehistoric times mentioned earlier – part of the 'better safe than sorry' thinking that our ancestors used to survive the many dangers that were around them.

In modern days, this pattern of thinking, which is common to all of us, is called 'confirmation bias'. Our brains automatically look for examples of things that confirm our threat beliefs – to make sure we are keeping ourselves 'safe' – and tend not to look too hard at the things that might contradict our threat beliefs – as this could confuse the matter and jeopardise our 'safety'.

CASE EXAMPLE: Michael

Since moving in to his new flat, Michael had been bothered by neighbours living next door. When he went in and out of his flat, he often saw groups of people who looked shifty and intimidating standing around. A few weeks after he had moved in to his flat, Michael was mugged on the way home from work by someone wearing a mask. He was understandably very shaken up by the event, so did not leave the house for the next couple of weeks. Michael wonders if his dodgy neighbours were behind the mugging. He starts to find it hard to sleep and does not like to answer the door.

Spending a lot of time awake in his flat on his own, Michael starts to notice noises through the walls, hears his neighbours talking and laughing and spots electrical points in his flat which look like they might have been tampered with. He sees all this as evidence that his belief must be true – his neighbours are trying to harm him. Understandably, Michael does not feel at all safe in his flat. He becomes constantly watchful and has little time for anything else.

Eventually Michael goes to stay with his mum in the next town. For a few days Michael feels better, but then after hearing laughter in his mum's back garden, he starts to become worried about her neighbours too, and his poor sleep returns. Soon he is so worried that he does not come out of his room any more, and stays up all night listening for noises. Sometimes when his mum brings him cups of tea, he finds himself worrying that these may be poisoned.

Michael's belief about not being safe started when he was mugged. His confirmation bias then used the noises and damaged electrical sockets in his flat as 'evidence' that his neighbours were trying to harm him. When he moved to his mum's house, hearing laughter in her garden triggered that threat belief again, and Michael changed his behaviour to try and make himself feel safer – by staying in his room. Instead of making him feel safer, staying in his room gave Michael more time to worry about his safety, and his attention became completely focused on checking for more evidence to back up the belief. Eventually, the threat belief became so strong that Michael started to feel unsafe around his own mum, who had never done anything to harm him.

The above example shows how a very strong threat belief might develop for anyone, and how important it is to examine our threat beliefs carefully. Doing this is not easy or comfortable, and it might make us feel more anxious. Remember, there is nothing to lose by thinking things through logically, and there may potentially be a lot to gain. If we have a strong threat belief, our brains will also have a strong 'confirmation bias', so we would need to be quite strict and logical as we examine our beliefs. Talking them through with someone we trust can be helpful.

The following exercise will give some prompts to help us while thinking the beliefs through. Whether the threat belief is about something or someone specific, or absolutely everybody, there are some questions we can ask ourselves to help work out whether there might be some confirmation bias happening for us.

If your beliefs are about something or someone specific, do you still feel very worried and watchful all the time, even when those particular people are not around or when you are in a different place? If so, are there any logical reasons for this? Write down what you have noticed.

....

....

....

....

....

....

If your beliefs are about everyone, is there a
reasonable way that everybody could be 'in on'
something except you? Is there a good reason why
they would go to so much trouble to fool you?
Would there not be an easier way to get what
they want? Is there anybody you can run these
questions by to help you make sense of things?
Write down your thoughts on all of this.

....

....

....

....

....

....

....

Well done for doing those exercises – it is not easy
thinking to do.

Having thought through the above questions and examined your threat beliefs very carefully and logically, do you think there might be some confirmation bias happening for you at the moment? Tick the box that best matches your thoughts:

	Yes/No
My beliefs make perfect logical sense – I can't see any evidence that confirmation bias is happening.	
My beliefs make a lot of sense but there might be *some* confirmation bias happening.	
I have *definitely noticed some confirmation bias* when I have looked carefully at my beliefs.	

9

Actively Considering Alternatives

As we noted in previous chapters, one of the factors that can lead to us putting too much certainty into a threat belief is the brain's tendency to *actively look for* evidence that backs up our beliefs, while at the same time *dismissing or ignoring* evidence that might disagree with it. This can lead to us jumping to conclusions about 'evidence' in one way or another. What can we do about this? One way is to purposefully generate as many possible alternatives as we can. This helps our brains think about our threat belief as one of many possible explanations, allowing us to make a more informed decision.

For example, Eric notices a lot of calls from a number he does not recognise on his phone this week. Because Eric's threat belief is that he may be being monitored by the police, he automatically thinks this is what is happening. Despite feeling anxious, he decides to sit down and write out all the other possibilities.

Problem:

Six calls in three days from a number I do not recognise

Possible explanations:

1. Being monitored by the police
2. My number has been sold to a datamining company
3. Someone I know is calling me from a new number
4. Someone I know has given someone my number for work
5. My home or car insurance might be up for renewal
6. My bank might be calling me about the loan I have applied for
7. My electricity company might be trying to sell me a smart meter again
8. My TV company might be trying to sell me a new package again
9. The gym might be calling me as I cancelled my direct debit

Eric goes one step further and puts all the alternatives into a pie chart (see page 68), **leaving his threat belief until last**. Eric remembers putting his telephone number on to a competition form he filled in a few weeks ago and so thinks it might be possible that his number got sold to a datamining company – he has heard about this happening to his cousin so assigns about 25 per cent to this. Now he stops to think about it, Eric wonders if he may have won the competition. He does not think this is very likely but adds a little slice to the pie chart as a possibility. Eric works his way through the other possibilities, thinking logically about which is more or less likely than the others, but not spend-ing too much time on each one as it is just a best logical guess.

As Eric deliberately left his threat belief until last to add to the pie chart, he consciously stopped himself from 'jumping to' that conclusion without consid-ering all the other possibilities. Eric reflects that if he had not done it this way, he would have given his threat belief 95 per cent of the pie.

Eric finds that doing this has reduced his anxiety quite a lot and decides to keep doing this exercise when something triggers a strong sense of worry about his threat belief.

Try and list some alternatives for the example below. Then divide up all the options in the pie chart to see how this might help Michael put his threat belief into perspective (see page 70).

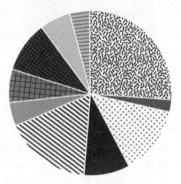

 My number has been sold to a data mining company

 I may have won the competition

 Someone I know is calling me from a new number

 Someone I know has passed on my number for work

 My home or car insurance might be up for renewal

 My bank might be calling me about that loan
I applied for

 My electricity company might be trying to sell me
a smart meter again

 My TV company might be trying to sell me a new
package again

 The gym might be calling me as I cancelled my
direct debit

 The police are monitoring me

Eric's pie chart

Michael hears people laughing as he walks out of his front door. Because his 'threat belief' is that people are trying to harm him, he automatically thinks this is what they are laughing about. What are some alternatives? List as many as you can and then add them to the blank pie chart. Give whatever percentage is left at the end to Michael's own threat belief – that people are trying to harm him.

....

....

....

....

....

....

....

Blank pie chart for Michael's situation

This is a strategy we can use for ourselves when we notice our threat belief getting triggered by an event or experience. You can use the blank table and pie on the next pages to keep a record, or draw your own. Get help doing this from someone you trust if it is hard to do on your own.

What was the situation?	What was the 'threat belief' you had?	List some alternative ways of looking at the situation

Blank pie chart

Actively considering alternatives should help you to feel less anxious in the short term, and as you gradually start to get your confidence back and challenge the threat beliefs, you may find day-to-day life becomes a little easier to cope with.

10

How Can I Help Myself in Future?

If you have found some of the exercises in the previous chapters helpful, you may already have started to notice that you are worrying a little less about some things that used to bother you a lot. How can you keep this change going and stop yourself slipping backwards? Bad days, bad weeks and even bad months happen to all of us, so it is important to be prepared. You may notice your old paranoid thoughts begin to get stronger again. Don't panic. Below are some strategies which may help you manage paranoid thoughts better in the future.

Know when your stress bucket is getting full

Reread the earlier sections focusing on stress. Getting to know the things that cause you stress, and recognising when your bucket is getting full, will be important for the future. The better you can get at recognising your own stress levels, the sooner you can act to look after yourself, make some changes or seek support. And when your stress is better managed, your paranoid thoughts will almost certainly reduce.

Revisit your cycle

Revisiting your threat beliefs cycle every so often can be very helpful. This can just be a quick check-in, giving you a chance to notice which threat beliefs might be present for you at the moment, where you are focusing your attention, how you are feeling, and how your behaviour may have changed. Getting this understanding can help you to make the necessary changes in order to break the cycle.

Practise good self-care

Taking care of ourselves is really important, especially at times of stress. It is at these times that we may notice that our usual routines start to slip, perhaps because we aren't feeling so good or are distracted by what else is going on in our lives. Being mindful of this is always helpful. Self-care is a necessity, not a luxury. Some of the things to consider are:

- Try and get enough sleep; ideally we need around 7–8 hours a night. (For more advice around sleep see pages 57–8.)

- Take care of the basics: continue to get up, get washed and dressed, and take care of your personal hygiene.

- Make sure you have eaten something and drunk some water.

- Take care of your physical needs or ailments; see your doctor for any ongoing concerns.

- Spend time outside if you can, and if not, open your curtains or blinds and open a window to get some fresh air.

- Get regular exercise, whether this is a walk or a weights session in the gym – whatever you enjoy doing to get active!

- Take time out: rest, recover, unwind. We all need time to recharge sometimes.

Get creative

Writing, drawing, painting, colouring, playing or composing music, crafting, sculpting, knitting, etc., all help distract you from the troublesome thoughts, but can also be relaxing and give you a sense of achievement.

Check in with others

When we start to struggle, we sometimes have a tendency to isolate ourselves from others or avoid seeing the people who are there to support us. It's really important to remember that there are people who can help us, whether these are friends, family members or professionals. Checking in with some-one when we start to notice that our threat beliefs are becoming active again could mean that we get support and reassurance sooner rather than later. This could help not only with paranoid thoughts, but also with stress levels.

What things might help you? Use this space to write down some ideas.

....

....

....

....

....

Who are the people who you could reach out to for support? Make sure you note down their contact details too.

....

....

....

....

....

....

Useful Resources

We hope that you have found this book helpful. If you want to explore further, or if you feel that a different approach might be more useful for you, there are other resources available.

Your GP or family doctor is a good port of call to ask about further professional input. Sometimes another health professional, such as a psychologist or trained nurse, may be able to help you to work through this book. Or it may be that you would benefit from more formal therapy; if you have enjoyed the approach used in this book, then CBT may be one therapy to explore further.

Here are some examples of further reading you might find useful:

Overcoming Paranoid and Suspicious Thoughts by Daniel Freeman, Philippa Garety and Jason Freeman (2016)

Think You're Crazy, Think Again by
Anthony Morrison, Julia Renton, Paul French
and Richard Bentall (2008)

You may also find some of the other titles in this self-help introductory series useful.

If you like the cognitive behavioural approach used in this book, and would be interested in finding a qualified therapist, the **BABCP** is a register of qualified professionals:

www.babcp.org.uk

Other useful organisations and websites:

Mind
A leading mental health charity in the UK.
www.mind.org.uk

Rethink Mental Illness
Offers advice and support to those experiencing mental health difficulties.
www.rethink.org

Overcoming Paranoid & Suspicious Thoughts

Do you often suspect the worst of others? Mild to moderate paranoia, or mistrust of other people, is on the increase, and although it may feel justifiable at the time, unfounded suspicions of this kind can make life a misery. Research says between 20 and 30 per cent of people in the UK frequently have suspicious or paranoid thoughts. This is the first self-help guide to coping with what can be a debilitating condition.

An Introduction to Coping with Anxiety

Practical support for how to overcome anxiety

Anxiety is one of the most common mental health conditions worldwide, affecting millions of people each year. But it can be treated effectively with cognitive behavioural therapy (CBT).

Written by experienced practitioners, this introductory book can help you if anxiety has become a problem. It explains what anxiety is and how it makes you feel when it becomes unmanageable or lasts for long periods of time. It will help you to understand your symptoms and is ideal as an immediate coping strategy and as a preliminary to fuller therapy. You will learn:

- What anxiety is and how it develops
- Physical symptoms to look out for
- How to spot and challenge thoughts that make you anxious
- Ways to change how you behave in order to reduce your feelings of anxiety

Overcoming Worry and Generalised Anxiety Disorder

2nd Edition

Up to 44 in every 1000 adults suffer from a condition known as Generalised Anxiety Disorder. This is much more than the normal worrying we all do – it can be a debilitating disorder leading to significant personal and social problems and sometimes financial loss.

The user-friendly, step-by-step approach explains why they worry, how to recognise what feeds it and develop effective methods of dealing with it. With each step the authors introduce new ideas that add to the picture of worry, and use questionnaires, exercises and tasks to help the reader understand and then challenge unhelpful habits and beliefs.